WILDLIFE IN BLOOM SERIES

Little Wolf

BY AUTHOR & CONSERVATIONIST

LINDA BLACKMOOR

ISBN: 979-8-9904465-6-4 (PRINT)

PUBLISHED BY QUILL PRESS. LINDA BLACKMOOR'S TITLES MAY BE
PURCHASED IN BULK FOR EDUCATIONAL, BUSINESS, FUNDRAISING, OR
SALES PROMOTIONAL USE. FOR INFORMATION, PLEASE EMAIL
HELLO@LINDABLACKMOOR.COM

FIRST PRINT EDITION: 2024

LINDA BLACKMOOR
WWW.LINDABLACKMOOR.COM

WOLF FACT #1

SPECIES

Wolves include several magical species: the gray wolf, red wolf, and Ethiopian wolf, each adapted to specific regions. The gray wolf includes species like the Arctic wolf and Mexican wolf, which inhabits North America, Europe, and Asia. The red wolf is critically endangered, found mainly in the southeastern U.S. In Ethiopia's highlands, the Ethiopian wolf sadly is Africa's most endangered carnivore.

WOLF FACT #2

HOWLS

Wolves communicate through the use of enchanting howls, sharp barks, terrifying growls, and soft whines, each sound serving a specific purpose. Howls can carry up to 10 miles in open terrain, helping locate pack members and warn rivals. Different vocalizations convey messages like signaling danger or coordinating hunts. Vocal communication is essential for maintaining pack cohesion.

WOLF FACT #3

STEALTH

Wolves are apex predators employing cooperation and stealth in hunting. They can run at incredible speeds up to 38 miles per hour but rely on endurance to pursue prey. Their sense of smell is 100 times more sensitive than humans', aiding in tracking over vast distances. A powerful bite force allows them to take down large animals like elk and moose, which serve as their primary food source.

WOLF FACT #4

PACKS

Wolves live in packs functioning as family units led by an alpha male and female. Packs usually consist of 5 to 10 members, including parents and offspring from multiple years. This social structure facilitates cooperative hunting, pup rearing, and territory defense. Hierarchies are established through complex social behaviors and communication within the pack.

WOLF FACT #5

FAMILY

Wolves have a strong family bond among the pack. Parents nurture their pups with care, teaching them the ways of the wild. Play is essential for wolf pups to learn hunting and social skills. Activities like chasing and wrestling develop physical coordination and strength. Adults participate in play to reinforce bonds and teach survival skills. Play behavior also establishes hierarchy and social dynamics.

WOLF FACT #6

SIGNALS

Wolves use diverse body language like facial expressions, tail positions, and posture to communicate. Raised hackles, the hairs on the back of their neck, indicate aggression, while a tucked tail shows submission. Scent marking with urine and feces defines territories and conveys reproductive status. These nonverbal cues maintain social order within the pack.

WOLF FACT #7

BALANCE

As keystone species, wolves regulate populations of herbivores like deer and elk, preventing overgrazing. Their presence promotes biodiversity by allowing vegetation to flourish, which benefits other wildlife. Wolves can indirectly affect rivers and streams by influencing grazing patterns. Their ecological role is crucial for healthy ecosystems. When the wolves disappear, the environment suffers.

JOURNEY

Wolves can travel up to an incredible 30 miles in a single day while hunting or seeking new territory. Wolves adapt to various terrains, including forests, mountains, deserts, and tundras. Dispersing wolves may journey hundreds of miles to find mates or establish new packs of their own. Territories range from 50 to over 1,000 square miles, depending on prey availability.

PUPS

Wolf pups are born blind and deaf, weighing about one pound. Their eyes open after 10 days, and they begin hearing sounds, starting to explore the den area. By three weeks, pups eat regurgitated meat provided by adult pack members. Play among wolf pups helps to develop hunting skills and social bonds, which they learn through their parents and siblings.

WOLF FACT #10

LEGENDS

Across cultures through the centuries, wolves have inspired legends. Wolves feature prominently in folklore and mythology worldwide. Native American legends often portray wolves as symbols of loyalty, wisdom, and courage. In Roman mythology, a she-wolf nurtured Romulus and Remus, the founders of Rome. These cultural stories reflect humanity's long-standing fascination with wolves.

WOLF FACT #11

SENSES

Wolves have acute senses; their hearing detects sounds up to six miles away in forests. Their excellent night vision, due to a high number of light-sensitive eye cells, aids nocturnal hunting. Their refined sense of smell can detect prey buried under snow or track scents days old. These magical senses make them effective predators and communicators.

WINTER

In cold climates, wolves grow double-layered coats with outer guard hairs and dense underfur. Fur-covered paws insulate against snow and ice, and specialized blood vessels prevent freezing. They can withstand temperatures as low as -40°F (-40°C). Wolves conserve energy by resting during severe weather. This helps them thrive in beautiful snowy landscapes.

WOLF FACT #13

BONDS

Wolves often form lifelong monogamous bonds, with the alpha pair leading the pack. Typically, only the alpha male and female breed, focusing resources on a single litter annually. Strong pair bonds contribute to pack stability and cooperative care of pups. Monogamy ensures genetic diversity by preventing inbreeding.

www.ingramcontent.com/pod-product-compliance
Lightning Source LLC
Chambersburg PA
CBHW060838270326

41933CB00002B/125